EXPLORING SCIENCE

# IGNEOUS ROCKS

## FROM FIRE TO STONE

BY DARLENE R. STILLE

Content Adviser: Lynn S. Fichter, Ph.D.,
Department of Geology/Environmental Science, James Madison University

Science Adviser: Terrence E. Young Jr., M.Ed., M.L.S.,
Jefferson Parish (Louisiana) Public School System

Reading Adviser: Rosemary G. Palmer, Ph.D.,
Department of Literacy, College of Education, Boise State University

**Compass Point Books** • Minneapolis, Minnesota

IGNEOUS ROCKS

Compass Point Books • 3109 West 50th Street, #115 • Minneapolis, MN 55410

Copyright© 2008 by Compass Point Books
All rights reserved. No part of this book may be reproduced without written permission from the publisher. The publisher takes no responsibility for the use of any of the materials or methods described in this book, nor for the products thereof.
Printed in the United States of America.

 This book was manufactured with paper containing at least 10 percent post-consumer waste.

Photographs ©: Corbis/Thinkstock, cover; Corbis/ORIETTA SCARDINO/epa, 4; Photo Researchers, Inc/Stephen & Donna O'Meara, 5; Photo Researchers, Inc/Bernhard Edmaier, 7; Corbis/Charles Bowman/Robert Harding World Imagery, 9; Photo Researchers, Inc/David Hardy, 10; Photo Researchers, Inc/Charles D. Winters, 11; Photo Researchers, Inc/Richard J. Green, 13; Geophysical Laboratory, Carnegie Institution of Washington, 14; Photo Researchers, Inc/Alfred Pasieka, 16; Photo Researchers, Inc/Mark A. Schneider, 17, 19 (top left, middle left, top center, middle center); Shutterstock/Paul Cowan, 18; Photo Researchers, Inc/Joyce Photographics, 19 (bottom left); Photo Researchers, Inc/Edward Kinsman, 19 (bottom middle); Photo Researchers, Inc/Andrew J. Martinez, 19 (top right); Shutterstock/wheatley, 19 (bottom right); Photo Researchers, Inc/George Whitely, 20; Photo Researchers, Inc/Dirk Wiersma, 21; Peter Arnold/Fritz Polking, 24; Photo Researchers, Inc/Gregory G. Dimijian, M.D., 25; Photo Researchers, Inc/Doug Martin, 26; Shutterstock/eric j enger, 27; Photo Researchers, Inc/Simon Fraser, 29; Shutterstock/FloridaStock, 33; Shutterstock/Bjartur Snorrason, 34; Shutterstock/Lee O'Dell, 35; Corbis/REUTERS/Sergei Karpukhin, 38; Shutterstock/Silvio Verrecchia, 39; Shutterstock/pmphoto, 40; Shutterstock/MalibuBooks, 42; Corbis/Akhtar Soomro/epa, 43; Shutterstock/Geoff Delderfield, 44; Corbis/Lester V. Bergman, 46.

Editor: Anthony Wacholtz
Designer: The Design Lab
Page Production: Lori Bye
Photo Researcher: Lori Bye
Illustrator: Ashlee Schultz

Creative Director: Keith Griffin
Editorial Director: Nick Healy
Managing Editor: Catherine Neitge

**Library of Congress Cataloging-in-Publication Data**
Stille, Darlene R.
 Igneous rocks : from fire to stone / by Darlene R. Stille ; illustrator, Ashlee Schultz.
       p. cm.—(Exploring science)
 Includes index.
 ISBN 978-0-7565-3252-9 (library binding)
 1. Rocks, Igneous—Juvenile literature. I. Schultz, Ashlee, ill. II. Title. III. Series.
 QE461.S747 2008
 552'.1—dc22                    2007032678

Visit Compass Point Books on the Internet at www.compasspointbooks.com or e-mail your request to custserv@compasspointbooks.com

### About the Author

Darlene R. Stille is a science writer and author of more than 80 books for young people. When she was in high school, she fell in love with science. While attending the University of Illinois, she discovered that she also loved writing. She was fortunate enough to find a career as an editor and writer that allowed her to combine both of her interests. Darlene Stille lives and writes in Michigan.

# TABLE OF CONTENTS

*c h a p t e r*                                                           *p a g e*

**1**    **HOW IGNEOUS ROCKS FORM** .................................................................... **4**

**2**    **MINERAL STEW** ........................................................................................ **11**

**3**    **GROUPING IGNEOUS ROCKS** ................................................................ **18**

**4**    **WHERE ON EARTH IGNEOUS ROCKS ARE FOUND** ............................ **27**

**5**    **IGNEOUS ROCKS IN THE ROCK CYCLE** ................................................ **36**

**6**    **HOW WE USE IGNEOUS ROCKS** ............................................................ **39**

*Glossary* .................................................................... 45

*Did You Know?* ........................................................ 46

*Further Resources* .................................................... 47

*Index* ........................................................................ 48

CHAPTER ONE

# How Igneous Rocks Form

**A TRICKLE OF MELTED ROCK** creeps down the side of a volcano. On top of the red-hot rock, a gray crust of cooling rock forms. A fountain of liquid rock spews out of another volcano and lights up the night sky. A wide river of fire flows down the mountainside, destroying roads, houses, and everything else in its path. From another volcano, a huge gray cloud spews forth and covers hundreds of square miles of land with a thick coating of ash and rock. All of these volcanoes are "factories" that create igneous rock.

During the evening, lava can easily be seen flowing down the side of Mount Etna near Catania, Italy. Europe's largest and most active volcano, Mount Etna erupts every few months.

# How Igneous Rocks Form

The word *volcano* has two meanings. It can mean the opening or vent where the magma, or molten rock, comes out. It can also mean the mountain that builds up around the vent.

There are three main types of rock on Earth: igneous, sedimentary, and metamorphic. The type of rock that comes out of volcanoes is igneous rock. *Igneous* is a word meaning "made from fire or heat."

All igneous rocks are formed deep inside Earth from magma. The magma contains hot gases that cause some volcanoes to erupt violently. The magma melts the rock above and pushes other rocks aside to form a space called a magma chamber. Sometimes the magma erupts from volcanoes. This magma is called lava. As it cools, lava forms a type of rock that geologists call volcanic rock. This rock is also called extrusive, which is a word meaning forced or pushed out.

Several streams of lava flowed into the Pacific Ocean near Hawaii, cooling the melted rock and setting off a series of steam "explosions."

# IGNEOUS ROCKS

Sometimes magma rises to just below Earth's surface and cools without erupting. This magma forms plutonic or intrusive rock.

The quick cooling of lava forms a type of igneous rock with particles, or grains, so tiny that they cannot be seen with the naked eye. Geologists call these rocks fine-grained, or aphanitic, rock. An example of this type of igneous rock is basalt.

Slow-cooling magma forms a type of igneous rock with grains large enough to be seen with the naked eye. Geologists call such rocks coarse-grained, or phaneritic, rock. An example of this type of igneous rock is granite.

## LAVA FLOWS AND PYROCLASTICS

Depending on how much gas it contains, magma erupts in one of two forms. If magma is low in gas, the eruption becomes a lava flow. Some lavas flow quickly, like syrup on pancakes. Other lavas hardly seem to move at all.

If magma contains a lot of gas, the eruption is like an

> **DID YOU KNOW?**
>
> Hawaii has several beaches of black sand. They were created by water breaking down basalt that hardened from lava.

explosion. This type of volcanic eruption is called a pyroclastic flow. Gas and dust blast out of the volcano in a huge, dark cloud containing water and pyroclastic pieces. The cloud hugs the ground like fog and moves very fast. The cloud is very hot and instantly burns everything in its path. It can rush over the ground at speeds up to 100 miles (160 kilometers) per hour.

In August 1997, pyroclastic flows from the Soufriere Hills volcano covered Plymouth, Montserrat Island, with ash and mud. The town's residents were evacuated before the volcano erupted.

## Types of Lavas

Lava has two basic forms, lava flows and pyroclastics. Which form the lava takes depends on the magma's viscosity—how runny or how thick and sticky it is. Lava that flows out of volcanoes varies in how easily it flows. Hot lava tends to be thin and runny, but as it cools, it gets thicker and slower. There are four basic types of lava flows that cool to form basalts—pahoehoe, a'a, pillow lava, and columnar lava.

Pahoehoe is the first type of lava to erupt from volcanoes such as those in Hawaii. It is smooth lava that cools to form various shapes, such as ropes. Sometimes the outside of pahoehoe cools to form a hollow lava tube. Red-hot lava flows inside the hollow tube. A'a lava follows pahoehoe. A'a is a cooler lava, and therefore much thicker. As it flows, it cracks and breaks into chunks that accumulate. These chunks pile upward and then tumble forward. Pillow lava forms when lava spills out under water or flows into water. For example, pillow lava is created when lava flows in Hawaii spill over the sea cliffs into the ocean. Pillow lavas form spheres or tube shapes. Columnar lava can form in lava that flows out like a sheet. When a sheet of thick lava cools, it shrinks and cracks into long vertical columns. One type of columnar lava, called columnar jointed lava, makes spectacular shapes. The Giant's Causeway in Ireland and Devil's Tower in Wyoming are famous

*How Igneous Rocks Form*

examples of columnar jointed lava.

On the other hand, pyroclastics form from thick, sticky lava that contains large amounts of gas. The gas causes the lava to explode out of a volcano. The blast breaks the lava into small pieces. The smallest pyroclastic pieces are ash. Ash is like a fine powder that blows out in clouds. Lapilli are somewhat larger pieces of lava, ranging from a peanut to a walnut in size. The largest pyroclastics are called blocks and bombs. Blocks are square or rectangular pieces of lava. Bombs are round or tube-shaped, and they are often twisted like taffy. The magma is still hot and able to mold into a different shape when it surfaces. As it spins, the lava develops a twist.

Weathering causes columnar lava to become six-sided, like honeycombs. Because of their hexagonal shape, the columns are packed closely together.

## POOLS OF IGNEOUS ROCK

Magma does not always erupt. Sometimes magma forces its way into spaces in and between rocks underground and forms sills. Magma that cuts across existing rock layers forms dikes. A laccolith is similar to a dike, but there is enough magma to push the ground upward, forming a flat-bottomed, upward-domed bulge at Earth's surface. Large bulges form batholiths that can become mountains.

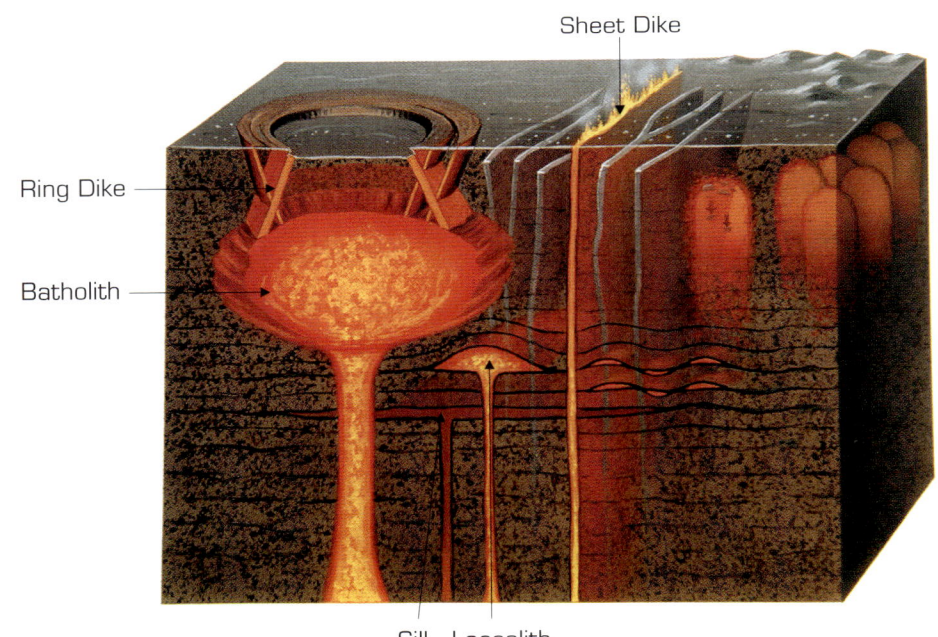

CHAPTER TWO

# Mineral Stew

**MAGMA THAT COOLS AND HARDENS** into igneous rock is like a mineral stew. Minerals—nonliving solids found in rocks and soil—are made of 92 chemical elements in nature. Chemical elements are made of tiny particles called atoms. Each chemical element is made up of one type of atom. The atoms that make up each element combine with other atoms in various ways to create about 3,000 kinds of minerals. Some elements, such as iron, nickel, silver, and gold, are also minerals. While beef stew contains carrots, potatoes, and other vegetables, this mineral stew contains quartz, feldspar, mica, and many other natural minerals. Igneous rocks are made of two or more minerals.

Magmas that rise to the surface at different places on Earth contain various mixes of minerals. Even though there are more than 3,000 minerals, most of them are rare. Earth's rocks are mainly made up of about 100 minerals, but igneous rocks are mostly made up of only eight minerals. Each of these

The mineral mica splits evenly into thin layers that are flexible but sturdy.

eight minerals falls into a certain category. These categories are mafic minerals (olivine, pyroxene, amphibole, and biotite), feldspars (plagioclase and orthoclase), micas (biotite and muscovite), and quartz. Biotite, which falls under two categories, is the only exception.

## BOWEN'S REACTION SERIES

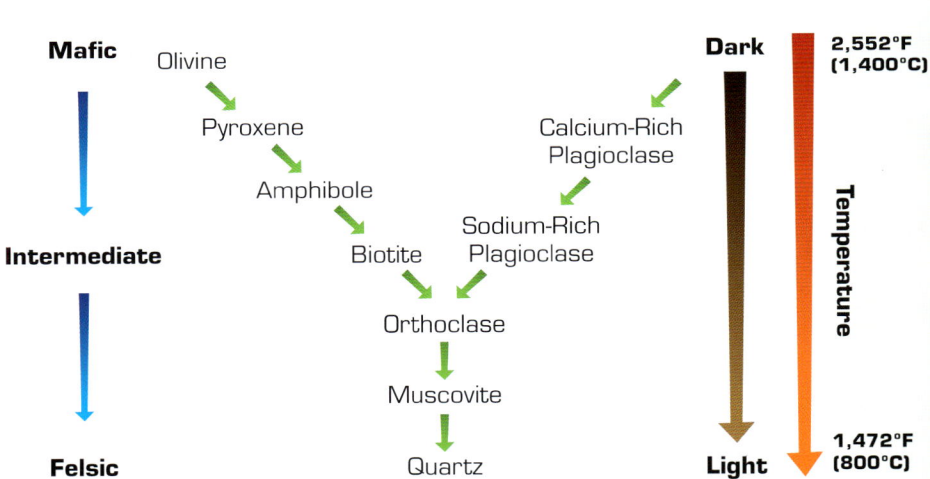

Bowen's reaction series categorizes the minerals that make up igneous rocks. They are grouped by the temperature at which the rocks formed, the type of magma the rocks formed from, and by the color of the rocks.

### Norman L. Bowen and Fractionation

One of the greatest mysteries in geology when Norman L. Bowen was a young man in the early 1900s was how granite formed. At that time, petrologists—scientists who study rocks—mainly went on rock-collecting trips with pickaxes, magnifying hand lenses, and notebooks. They studied the minerals in various types of rocks and noted where they were found. Using these tools, petrologists learned a great deal about rocks, but they could not figure out where granite, which is the foundation of continents, came from.

Bowen had an idea. Scientists used laboratory experiments to study other things, so why not rocks? Using a small electric furnace, he heated various mineral mixtures found in rocks, and then he cooled them again. He found that cycles of heating and partial melting followed by cooling again can result in the formation of different types of rocks.

This study proved that a variety of igneous rocks can form from a single magma. Bowen concluded that igneous rocks evolve, or change, and he based the vertical structure of his reaction series on this concept. All the kinds of rock on Earth evolved from a single type of "parent rock." The parent rock first came together when our planet formed from gas and dust that was swirling around the sun. The spinning young planet grew larger and hotter. The minerals that make up the various

*continued from page 13*

types of igneous rock "settled out" from the magma at different pressures and temperatures in a process known as fractionation. Over billions of years, the igneous rocks eroded and reformed, creating the other main rock types—sedimentary and metamorphic rocks.

Bowen's concept that rocks evolve by fractionation is one of the most important ideas in all of geology. Igneous rock fractionation means dividing a rock with one composition into fractions, or parts—each with a different composition.

Imagine a glass jar filled with two kinds of candy that melt at different temperatures. When the jar is heated, the candy with the lowest melting point melts to form a liquid, but the higher-melting-point candy remains solid. If the melted candy is poured out of the jar, leaving behind the solid candy, the two candies have been fractionated. Igneous rocks fractionate the same way.

In 1928, Norman L. Bowen (1887–1956) wrote *The Evolution of the Igneous Rocks*, which became a standard classification textbook for petrologists.

*Mineral Stew*

The two most common elements in igneous rock minerals are oxygen and silicon. Together, these elements account for almost 94 percent of the volume of Earth's crust and half of its weight. Rocks containing these two elements are called silicates, which make up 95 percent of all the rocks on Earth. Other common elements found in rock minerals are magnesium, iron, calcium, sodium, and potassium.

### MINERAL CRYSTALS

When magma cools, its minerals form crystals, which are orderly arrangements of atoms in a pattern that repeats over and over again. These crystals form shapes that stack up in an orderly pattern that can be very beautiful. One way rock collectors can tell minerals apart is by the shape of their crystals.

Regardless of magma type, the size of the crystals depends on the rate of cooling. Rocks that form inside Earth—where the cooling magma is insulated and cools slowly—develop large crystals. Rocks that form at Earth's surface—where

**DID YOU KNOW?**

Most quartz crystals are transparent, which means you can see through them. Some quartz crystals are so clear they are used for lenses in microscopes.

cooling is relatively rapid—develop crystals that are usually too small to be seen by the naked eye.

## RECIPE FOR ROCKS

Pick up a rock and feel whether it is rough or smooth. Look at its color. Rocks can be brown, red, gray, black, yellow, white, or a mixture of many colors. Some rocks are dull, and others sparkle. How a rock looks and feels depends on the minerals it contains.

Amethyst crystals, which are often used in jewelry, are a variety of quartz.

*Mineral Stew*

There are various kinds of minerals in the igneous rocks of Earth's crust and the magma of the mantle. Minerals called feldspars make up about 60 percent of the igneous rocks in Earth's crust. The most common minerals in the magma in Earth's mantle belong to the olivine group. Olivines are green or greenish-yellow minerals that are rich in iron and magnesium. Other important rock-forming minerals in the mantle are pyroxenes and amphiboles.

Green olivine crystals within a volcanic basalt bomb

CHAPTER THREE

# Grouping Igneous Rocks

**GEOLOGISTS HAVE MANY WAYS** of grouping igneous rocks. The most important is based on the composition of the rocks—either their chemistry (how much silica, oxygen, iron, calcium, etc., they have) or the minerals that make them up. Composition is important because it tells geologists where the magmas came from in Earth and how the rock evolved, or changed, with time.

The most common way to show igneous rock composition is by using Bowen's reaction series. No igneous rock contains all the minerals in this series. Instead, rocks are divided into four kinds of magma, each with a different composition. Geologists call the magmas mafic, intermediate, felsic, and ultramafic. In addition to having a different chemistry and mineral makeup, each magma differs in how easily it flows when coming out of a volcano. The color of the rock that forms when the magma crystallizes also differs.

A second way of classifying igneous rocks is based on where they form. A rock can be either volcanic, meaning that it formed above the surface, or it can be plutonic, meaning that it formed under Earth's crust. All

Igneous rocks have a variety of characteristics, such as composition, that petrologists use to classify them.

*Grouping Igneous Rocks*

four magma types can form either below the surface or at the surface. Although the chemistry and mineral content of each magma do not vary depending on where it formed, the size of

## A CLASSIFICATION OF IGNEOUS ROCKS

| | | Cooling History/Texture | | |
|---|---|---|---|---|
| | | Slow-Cooling and Coarse-Grained | Fast-Cooling and Fine-Grained | Very Fast-Cooling and Glassy/Cellular |
| Composition/Color | Mafic and Dark Color | Gabbro | Basalt | Scoria |
| | Intermediate and Intermediate Color | Diorite | Andesite | |
| | Felsic and Light Color | Granite | Rhyolite | Pumice |

the crystals does vary. This means the rock's texture and name vary as well.

Mafic rocks are found at the top of Bowen's reaction series. The word *mafic* is a combination of "magnesium" and "ferrum"—a Latin word meaning "iron." Mafic magma does not contain much silicate, but it is rich in calcium, iron, and magnesium. These elements give minerals in mafic rocks, such as olivine, pyroxene, and calcium plagioclase, a dark color. Basalt is a fine-grained rock formed from mafic magma. Gabbro is an example of a coarse-grained rock formed from mafic magma.

At the bottom of Bowen's reaction series are felsic rocks.

Felsic is a name that combines two words: "feldspar" and "silica." Felsic magmas are rich in silicate and feldspar. They are thick and contain large amounts of sodium, aluminum, and potassium. Felsic magma is thicker than mafic magma, and the rocks it forms are usually light in color. These rocks make up the continents. Either

The felsic mineral muscovite, or white mica, is the most plentiful form of mica. It is commonly used in construction for fireproofing and insulation.

volcanic or plutonic igneous rocks can form from felsic magmas. Rhyolite forms from felsic lava that erupts from volcanoes. Granite forms from felsic magma that cools under the crust.

Intermediate magma has a chemical makeup between that of mafic and felsic. The rocks it produces have some characteristics of both mafic and felsic rocks. Intermediate igneous rocks can be classified as high- or low-intermediate. High-intermediate rocks, such as diorite and andesite, form at higher temperatures than low-intermediate rocks, such as granodiorite and dacite. More quartz is present in low-intermediate rocks than in high-intermediate rocks. In the way the coarse-grained gabbro has a fine-grained partner (basalt), the high- and low-intermediate rocks diorite and granodiorite have fine-grained partners: andesite and dacite.

Ultramafic magma is different from the other three types.

Komatiite is a rare ultramafic rock that forms from rapid crystallization.

Unlike mafic, intermediate, or felsic magma, ultramafic magma does not contain any feldspar. It also contains less silicate than other types of magma, but it is rich in minerals such as olivine and pyroxene.

## SLOW-COOLING PLUTONIC ROCKS

Plutonic rocks can be felsic, intermediate, or mafic. Gabbro is a mafic plutonic rock that contains mainly pyroxene and calcium plagioclase. It is related to basalt, and it has dark colors that range from dark green-gray to black. Because it is slow-cooling, it has large, coarse crystals.

Diorite is a high-intermediate plutonic rock. It is a very hard type of rock, mostly made of fairly equal amounts of sodium plagioclase and amphibole. Because the mix of minerals is black and white, the rock has a "salt and pepper" look. Diorite is similar to andesite, but it is slow-cooling and has larger grains.

Granodiorite is a light-colored, low-intermediate plutonic rock that has a lot of quartz and two kinds of feldspars: sodium-rich plagioclase and potassium-rich orthoclase. On the other hand, because it is so low in Bowen's reaction series, mafic minerals make up only a few percent of the total rock. Granodiorite is a low-intermediate rock because it contains quartz. It is often found along with granite in mountains.

*Grouping Igneous Rocks*

Pegmatite is one of the last rocks to form from slowly cooling magma. As a result, the crystals in pegmatite form at relatively low temperatures. Pegmatite contains large amounts of water vapor and fluorine gas. When the gas escapes, it

The Half Dome at Yosemite National Park in California consists of the plutonic rock granodiorite.

# IGNEOUS ROCKS

leaves pockets in the pegmatite where beautiful gems such as topaz and garnet form.

Granites are a common type of rock on continents made by intrusive magma after it slowly cools in underground chambers. Granite is a felsic rock that contains quartz, feldspar, and mica. These rocks contain very little of the darker mafic minerals, however, which is why they are so light in color. Granite has the same makeup as fast-cooling rhyolite. The slow-cooling minerals in granite form large crystals, which are easy to see. The crystals can be different colors, from black and light gray to white and pink. Granite is a very hard rock. Many mountains are made of granite and other intermediate and felsic rocks.

Granite rocks along a coastline in Acadia National Park in Maine

## FAST-COOLING VOLCANIC ROCKS

Volcanic rocks can also be mafic, intermediate, or felsic. Basalts are the most common type of igneous rock that cools fast from extrusive magma. Basalts are mafic rocks. As lava, basalts flow out quickly, and their appearance depends on how the lava cooled. Some basalts look like sponges because escaping gas in the magma created many holes. Others look like pleated cloth or bread dough because the pahoehoe lava wrinkled up in folds as it flowed out of the vent. Basalt is made of the minerals calcium, plagioclase, olivine, and pyroxene. Most basalts are black, but some are dark gray, red, brown, or even green.

Andesite is an intermediate volcanic rock that is more than half silicate. Andesite contains amphibole, plagioclase, and pyroxene. As lava, andesite is very thick. It often explodes out of volcanoes in huge gray clouds and forms pyroclastic flows.

Rhyolite is a felsic volcanic rock. It contains quartz, feldspar, and mica. Because it cools quickly, it is a fine-grained rock.

A black-sand beach in Kamoamoa, Hawaii, formed from the erosion of basalt in the ocean. The sand was brought ashore by ocean waves to form a dark coastline.

IGNEOUS ROCKS

## VERY FAST-COOLING ROCKS

Scoria is a very fast-cooling rock that is like a glass. Scoria can come from either mafic or intermediate lava. Gases trapped in the lava create large holes in the rock.

Pumice is a very fast-cooling felsic rock that is related to granite and rhyolite. It is a white or cream-colored rock that is full of holes and looks foamy. Lava that cooled into pumice was filled with gases. Once the gases escape, the rock is so light and full of holes that it can float.

Obsidian is a natural glass. It is created by lava that cools very fast. It cools so fast that crystals do not have time to form. Instead, the lava becomes a smooth, natural glass that is usually black. Although it contains elements that give it a dark color, obsidian is a felsic rock that is closely related to two light-colored rocks: slow-cooling granite and fast-cooling rhyolite.

Because obsidian lacks a crystal structure, it can be "knapped," or broken, into curved slivers with sharp edges by striking it with a hard object.

CHAPTER FOUR

# Where on Earth Igneous Rocks Are Found

**IGNEOUS ROCKS ARE FOUND** at various places on Earth. Granites and intermediate plutonic rocks like diorite and granodiorite form the bases of continents. They are usually found deep below the surface, buried under layers of sedimentary rocks. Therefore, in most places, the rocks are not visible. Sometimes the formation of mountains lifts the granites, diorites, and granodiorites, and erosion strips off the overlying sedimentary layers, making these rocks visible. In the western United States, the Sierra Nevada are composed mostly of white diorites and white granites. Pikes Peak in the Colorado Rocky

Pikes Peak, a part of the Colorado Rocky Mountain range, reaches 14,110 feet (4,304 meters) above sea level at its highest point.

# IGNEOUS ROCKS

Mountains is made of pink granite, and the Blue Ridge Mountains in the East are composed of granites and granodiorites.

Basalt, a volcanic mafic rock, is the main type of rock on the floor of the world's oceans. Geologists have discovered why certain types of rocks occur in certain places. The reason stems from the fact that Earth's crust is made of many pieces called plates that float on the underlying mantle.

## TECTONIC PLATES

Earth's crust is broken into huge pieces called tectonic plates. These plates slide around on the hot, melted rock of the mantle, in the way ice slabs float on a lake and jostle against each other. The places where two plates meet are called plate boundaries. In some places, the plates move apart. This is called a divergent boundary. Under the Atlantic Ocean, two plates are pulling apart. The area where the plates are separating is called the Mid-Atlantic Ridge. In the gap between the plates, magma rises and lava pours out of volcanic vents in the seafloor. The quick-cooling lava creates pillow basalt. As more lava pours out, the basalt builds up to form new crust and an underwater mountain range.

In other places, known as convergent boundaries, the plates collide, and subduction occurs—when one plate slips under the edge of another. This happens when a heavier

oceanic plate of mafic rocks collides with a lighter oceanic plate. The heavier plate slips under the lighter plate. If the oceanic plate converges on a continent, then the heavy, mafic oceanic plate slips under the lighter continent, which is made of granite.

In Pingvellir, Iceland, cliffs mark the Atlantic Fault, where the North American and European tectonic plates are slowly moving apart.

> **DID YOU KNOW?**
>
> There are 14 large tectonic plates, as well as numerous smaller plates. The plates are named after the continents or bodies of water they carry, such as the Pacific plate and the African plate.

For example, the eastern edge of the Pacific plate is slipping under the western edge of the North American plate. As it sinks down into the mantle, the edge of the Pacific plate melts and becomes part of the mantle's magma. At the same time, some of the mantle above the subducted plate partially melts, and magma is sent toward the surface, creating the Cascade volcanic chain. As the heavier oceanic plate continues to subduct, though, the area of the ocean on the surface becomes smaller and smaller. This is called a remnant ocean basin because as it gets smaller, it becomes a remnant of its former, larger self. Eventually, when all the oceanic plate has subducted, the continents on the opposite sides of the completely subducted ocean collide, crumple up, and form mountain ranges. The Alps in Europe and the Himalayas in Asia were formed by colliding continental plates.

All around the rim of the Pacific Ocean, ocean plates are subducting. This means the entire rim of the Pacific Ocean

*Where on Earth Igneous Rocks Are Found*

is lined with volcanoes—they are in the Andes in South America, the Cascades in North America, the Aleutian Islands off Alaska, Japan in the western Pacific, and other areas. This is why the Pacific rim is called the Ring of Fire—the ocean is surrounded by volcanoes.

In still other places, called transform boundaries, the plates grind past one another. When this happens, no land is created or lost.

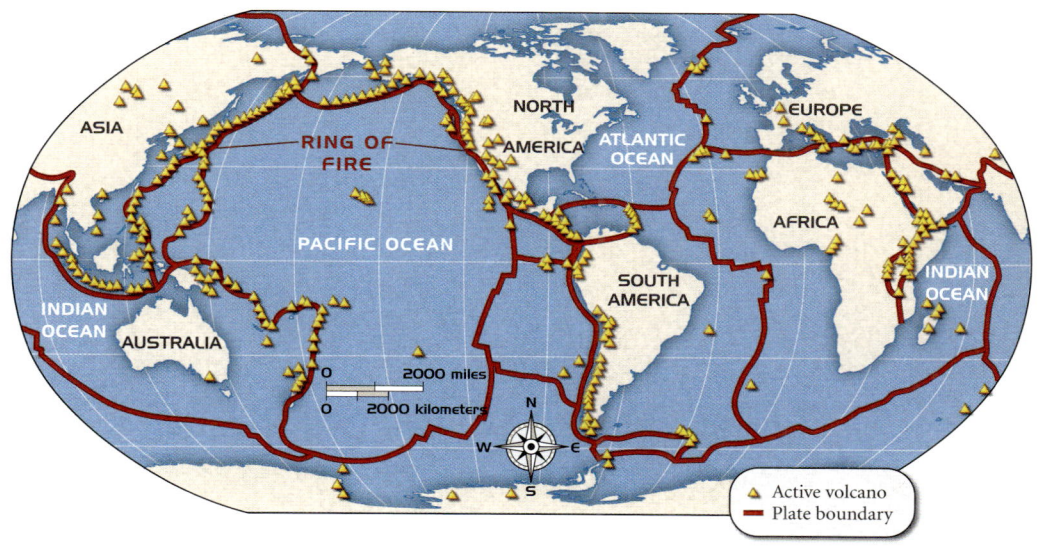

The Ring of Fire lies on the boundaries of the Pacific plate.

## THE PLATES AND THE MAGMAS

Particular types of magma and rocks are found at particular places in and under Earth's crust. Mafic materials are usually found where two tectonic plates are spreading apart and forming new ocean basins. Mafic magmas ooze out of volcanic vents in the seafloor. Mafic magma that erupts and cools quickly forms basalt. Below the surface, the more slowly cooling mafic magma forms gabbro.

Intermediate magma forms when the edge of a plate sinks beneath another plate and melts. Intermediate magma, for example, collects in chambers near the western edge of the North American plate. The lava blasts out of volcanoes as andesites and pumice, which form ash clouds and pyroclastic flows. Intermediate magma that cools underground forms diorite. Intermediate magma created the Cascade Range, with such famous peaks as Mount Rainier and Mount St. Helens—part of the Ring of Fire.

Both felsic and intermediate magmas are found where tectonic plates are converging. Eruptions of felsic volcanoes on continents are very rare. Scientists estimate that they occur once every million years, which is a good thing, because they erupt with a violent blast. Geologists call them supervolcanoes. Felsic magma boils in a huge chamber under Yellowstone National Park. The Yellowstone supervolcano erupted

three times in the past—2.1 million, 1.3 million, and 640,000 years ago. Geologists wonder not whether it will erupt again—only when.

Ultramafic magma remains mainly in the mantle. Ultramafic rocks are very rare in the crust. The most common ultramafic rock is peridotite.

### ROCKS FROM HOT SPOTS

Hot spots are places where hot magma blasts up through tectonic plates like a blowtorch. Geologists believe that these hot spots come from deep within Earth. A hot spot under the

At 14,410 feet (4,395 m) above sea level, Mount Rainier is the tallest mountain (and volcano) in the state of Washington.

Pacific plate created the Hawaiian Islands. Mafic lava from this hot spot built volcanic mountains of basalt on the seafloor. The mountains grew higher and higher until they rose above the ocean. The Hawaiian Islands are the tops of a long string of these volcanoes. As the plate passed over the hot spot, a series of islands formed.

Geologists believe that a hot spot is responsible for the magma under Yellowstone National Park. Still, the origin of its magma is a little more complicated. The Yellowstone hot spot pools mafic magma deep below the surface, at the base of the continent. The resulting heat melts the lower part of the continent, which is felsic in composition. Then this felsic magma works its way to the surface to

Iceland's Lakagigar was created by a series of volcanic eruptions. Each eruption occured north of the previous eruptions.

erupt as the volcano. Because the volcano is made from felsic magma, granites are slowly cooling far below the surface. At the surface, rhyolites, obsidian, and pumice are present. Today the volcano is dormant, or "sleeping," but heat from the cooling magma below the surface heats the water to form geysers, such as the famous Old Faithful. Hot springs and boiling mud pots form in the same way.

Old Faithful in Yellowstone National Park shoots water 120 to 150 feet (37 to 46 m) in the air. Erupting every 30 to 120 minutes, the geyser has not missed an eruption in 80 years.

CHAPTER FIVE

## Igneous Rocks in the Rock Cycle

**EARTH RECYCLES EVERYTHING.** Water is constantly recycled—from bodies of water to clouds in the sky to rain and snow that falls or drains back into bodies of water. Gases in the atmosphere are recycled into plants and animals and eventually back into the atmosphere. Mountains, however, are made of massive blocks of solid granite. How can granite be recycled?

The rock cycle begins when heat and pressure create the "mineral stew" inside Earth. Lava flows or blasts from volcanoes to create granite, basalt, and other igneous rocks. Weathering by wind, water, and atmospheric gases breaks the hard rock into smaller pieces. The smallest pieces form sand and soil particles.

Wind and water move particles of sand and soil into lakes and rivers. The particles form sediments at the bottoms of these bodies of water. Over millions of years, the layers of sediments harden into sedimentary rocks.

Meanwhile, tectonic plates that carry the oceans and continents keep moving. At certain places, the edges of two plates that are coming together eventually meet. The edge of one plate plunges beneath the other. The edge of the plunging oceanic plate melts, sending magma up toward the surface. For example, where the Pacific plate meets the North American plate, the magma begins to rise under the North American plate. The great heat and pressure from this rising magma alter the sedimentary rock it

## Igneous Rocks in the Rock Cycle

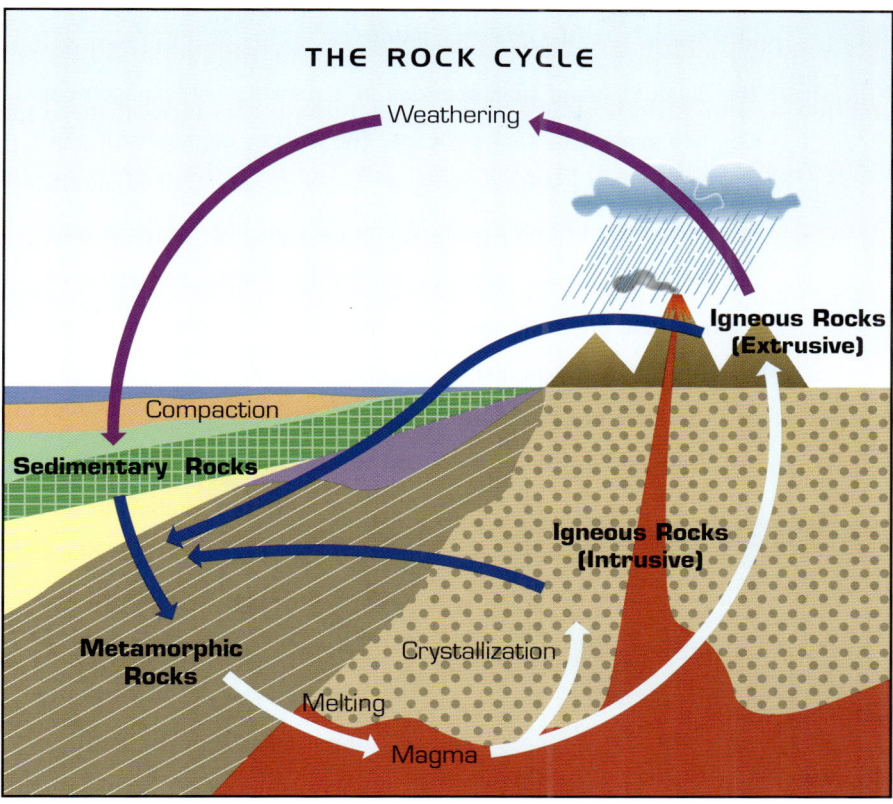

passes through, creating yet another rock type called metamorphic rock. The magma rises to the surface and blasts out as pyroclastic lava, which cools to form igneous rock. Erosion exposes the igneous rock, and the rock cycle begins all over again, with the rocks changing composition, or evolving, during the entire process.

## Diamonds and Igneous Rock

The clear diamond that sparkles in a necklace or engagement ring has made a fantastic voyage. The journey began about 100 miles (161 km) down, inside Earth's mantle, and took hundreds of millions of years. Diamonds are not an igneous rock, but without igneous rock we would never get diamonds. Diamonds are made of the chemical element carbon. High temperatures and high pressures in the mantle cause the carbon there to form the crystals that are diamonds.

Diamonds are carried to Earth's surface by igneous rocks called kimberlite and lamproite. The kimberlite or lamproite formed from magma that traveled upward through the mantle and crust. The lava in the pipe erupted as a volcano, throwing out diamonds along with the lava that formed igneous rocks. Diamonds are found in many places, including North and South America, India, Russia, and Australia.

Many large kimberlite pipes in Russia are the country's main source of diamonds.

CHAPTER SIX

# How We Use Igneous Rocks

**IGNEOUS ROCKS HAVE A WIDE RANGE OF** uses. They are used in construction, manufacturing, and in many other ways. You might find igneous rocks in your home. They can show up in kitchens as countertops. They can show up in bathrooms or entryways as floor tile. They can show up in gardens as landscape rock. They can even show up in cleaning products.

Hard igneous rocks are essential in construction. The igneous rock is cut from quarries. Granite, rhyolite, basalt, gabbro, and other igneous rocks can be crushed into gravel for the construction industry. The gravel can be used to form railroad track beds or as support under the concrete of highways. Igneous rocks are also ingredients in concrete.

Granite, one of the hardest rocks, is an important building material. Machines cut big blocks of granite from quarries in New Hampshire

Rocks and gravel are used as a base under railroad tracks to absorb the movement of the train over a larger area. They also allow water to drain properly from the railroad ties.

39

IGNEOUS ROCKS

and other Eastern states. In fact, New Hampshire's nickname is "The Granite State." The surfaces of granite blocks and slabs can be polished to a shine. The coarse grains make beautiful patterns. Polished granite is used for monuments and for the fronts of buildings. It is also a popular material for countertops in kitchens and bathrooms.

Rhyolite has many of the same uses as granite. Because it has finer grains than granite, a polished rhyolite surface usually does not have patterns. It is more likely to be a solid color. It is used for countertops, in landscaping, and for the facings of buildings and other structures.

Polished slabs of gabbro are sometimes sold as "black granite," a strange name to a geologist since real granite is always light-colored. These dark slabs are often used as memorial markers on graves in cemeteries.

Mount Rushmore was carved out of a large granite cliff in South Dakota. The heads of former Presidents George Washington, Thomas Jefferson, Theodore Roosevelt, and Abraham Lincoln are 60 feet (18 m) tall.

40

Because of its smooth texture, basalt is popular with sculptors and carvers. From ancient times, basalt has been carved to make stone weapons, figurines, and other decorative objects.

## MANUFACTURING

Igneous rocks have a range of uses in manufacturing various products. Pumice is an important abrasive. It is used in processes that involve grinding or polishing. It is also used in the textile industry for stone-washing jeans and other denim products. Pieces of pumice and dyed denim go into big washing vats. As the denim tumbles around in the water, the pumice rubs on the fabric. This action gives the denim a worn look. It also softens the fabric. Ground-up pumice might be in the cleaner you use on your sink or the file you use to trim your fingernails. Pumice is also used to make sandpaper.

The fiberglass insulation in your house might not be glass at all. It might be basalt. To make basalt into "glass" fibers, the stone is first crushed. The crushed basalt is melted in a furnace. Basalt melts at a low temperature because it is high in silicates. Material melted to make ordinary glass also contains mainly silicates. A machine pulls the basalt into thin strands as it cools. The fibers can be used in the textile industry or made into fiberglass insulation for homes, offices, and schools.

## Igneous Kitchen Countertops

Because granite is very hard and durable, many people want granite countertops in their kitchens. In addition, granite is a beautiful rock. Large and small mineral crystals that form as the underground magma slowly cools create interesting patterns in the granite. There are many colors of granite to choose from.

Many granites get their color from the mineral tourmaline, which appears in a range of colors, depending on what elements it contains. Iron gives tourmaline a black, brown, or dark blue color. Magnesium in tourmaline can make the granite brown or yellow. Lithium in tourmaline can result in a variety of colors, including reds and pinks.

Black countertops are very popular. Black stone countertops are not usually granite. Countertops with small crystals are made of basalt. Coarser-grained "black granite" countertops are made from gabbro.

Many contemporary kitchens feature polished granite.

## OTHER USES

Many gemstones are found in igneous rock. They are used to make bracelets, necklaces, rings, and other jewelry. Zircon, topaz, and ruby form in various types of volcanic rocks. Emeralds, garnets, and tourmaline form in pegmatite, a type of intrusive igneous rock. Peridot forms in magma in the mantle.

Glassy obsidian can be cut and polished to make necklaces, earrings, and other jewelry. It is also used to

Many types of quartz, along with other minerals, such as topaz, ruby, and emerald, are used to create an assortment of beautiful rings.

make surgical instruments. Obsidian makes very thin, sharp scalpels for surgery.

Some igneous rocks contain deposits of valuable ores. For example, the coarse-grained mafic rock anorthosite sometimes contains titanium ore. Also, peridotite contains chromium ore.

Igneous rocks are not only for making mountains and seafloors. They also can be found in many important products that we use every day.

An artistic wall made of igneous rocks

# GLOSSARY

**basalt**—main type of igneous rock in the oceans that cools from lava

**chemical elements**—substances made of a single type of atom

**crystals**—minerals with an orderly arrangement of atoms

**extrusive rocks**—rocks made from magma that erupts from volcanoes and cools rapidly; also called volcanic rock

**granite**—main type of igneous rock made from cooling felsic magma trapped underground on the continents

**intrusive rocks**—rocks made from magma that slowly cooled underground; also called plutonic rock

**lava**—magma that comes out of a volcano

**magma**—hot, molten rock

**minerals**—nonliving solids made of chemical elements

**petrologists**—scientists who study rocks

**pyroclastic flow**—magma containing large amounts of gas that blasts out of a volcano in clouds of ash and rock

**silicates**—most common minerals in igneous rocks; made of silicon and oxygen bound by metals such as iron, magnesium, and calcium

**tectonic plates**—giant plates that make up Earth's crust

**volcanoes**—vents in Earth's crust from which lava pours; mountains formed from the buildup of lava

D I D   Y O U   K N O W ?

- Astronauts who landed on the moon collected rocks that turned out to be basalts. This told scientists that the moon once had volcanoes that erupted and sent out hot lava.

- The 1980 eruption that blew away the side of Mount St. Helens in Washington state was a pyroclastic flow.

- Native Americans used a process called "flintknapping" to create knives and arrowheads from pieces of obsidian. They chipped at the obsidian with pieces of rock or other tools to create sharp edges on the glassy material.

- Diamonds are so rare that only about 0.07 ounces (2 grams) of them are found in every 100 tons (90 metric tons) of rock.

- Crystals that make up igneous rocks appear in all sizes. Some crystals can become huge. One of the largest known crystals, made of the mineral beryl, measured 59 feet (18 m) by 11½ feet (3.5 m) and weighed about 837,750 pounds (376,988 kilograms).

Because of their unique crystallization process, magnesium crystals can have a featherlike appearance.

# FURTHER RESOURCES

## Further Reading

Dussling, Jennifer A. *Looking at Rocks*. New York: Grosset & Dunlap, 2001.
Harman, Rebecca. *Rock Cycles*. Chicago: Heinemann Library, 2005.
Stewart, Melissa. *Igneous Rocks*. Chicago: Heinemann Library, 2002.
Symes, R.F. *Rocks & Minerals*. New York: DK Publishing, 2004.

## On the Web

For more information on this subject, use FactHound.
1. Go to *www.facthound.com*
2. Type in this book ID: **0756532523**
3. Click on the *Fetch It* button.
FactHound will find the best Web sites for you.

## On the Road

University of Wisconsin
Geology Museum
1215 W. Dayton St.
Madison, WI 53706
608/262-1412

The Gottesman Hall of Planet Earth
Halls of Minerals and Gems
American Museum of Natural History
Central Park West and 79th Street
New York, NY 10024
212/769-5100

## Explore all the Earth Science books

**Erosion:** How Land Forms, How It Changes

**The Greenhouse Effect:** Warming the Planet

**Igneous Rocks:** From Fire to Stone

**Metamorphic Rocks:** Recycled Rock

**Minerals:** From Apatite to Zinc

**Natural Resources:** Using and Protecting Earth's Supplies

**Plate Tectonics:** Earth's Moving Crust

**Sedimentary Rocks:** A Record of Earth's History

**Soil:** Digging Into Earth's Vital Resource

A complete list of Exploring Science titles is available on our Web site: *www.compasspointbooks.com*

# INDEX

a'a lava flows, 8
amphiboles, 17
andesite, 19, 21, 25, 32
anorthosite, 44
aphantic rock. *See* fine-grained rock.
ash, 4, 9, 32
atoms, 11, 15

basalt, 6, 8, 19, 20, 25, 28, 39, 41, 42
batholiths, 10
biotite, 12
blocks, 9
bombs, 9
Bowen, Norman L., 13
Bowen's reaction series, 12, 18, 20, 22

calcium, 15, 18, 20, 22, 25
carbon, 38
classification chart, 19
coarse-grained rock, 6, 20, 21, 40, 42, 44
columnar lava flows, 8–9
composition, 14, 18, 34, 37
convergent boundaries, 28–29
crust, 15, 17, 18, 28, 32, 33, 38
crystals, 15–16, 18, 22, 23, 26, 38

dacite, 21
diamonds, 38
dikes, 10
diorite, 19, 21, 27, 32
divergent boundaries, 28

elements, 11, 15, 38, 42
erosion, 14, 27, 37
extrusive rock. *See* volcanic rock.

feldspar, 12, 17, 20, 22, 24
felsic rock, 18, 20, 21, 22, 25, 26, 32, 34–35
fine-grained rock, 6, 20, 21, 25
fractionation, 14

gabbro, 19, 20, 22, 32, 39, 40–41, 42
gemstones, 24, 43
geysers, 35
granite, 6, 19, 21, 24, 27, 28, 39–40, 42
granodiorites, 21, 22, 27, 28

high-intermediate rock, 21, 22
hot spots, 33–35

intermediate lava, 26
intermediate magma, 18, 21, 32
intermediate plutonic rock, 22, 27
intermediate volcanic rock, 25
intrusive rock. *See* plutonic rock.
iron, 17, 20

kimberlite, 38

laccoliths, 10
lamproite, 38
lava, 5, 6, 8–9, 21, 25, 26, 28, 32, 34, 36, 37, 38
lithium, 42
low-intermediate rock, 21, 22

mafic rock, 12, 18, 20, 22, 25, 26, 32, 34, 44
magma, 5–6, 8, 9, 10, 11, 13, 15, 17, 18–20, 21, 28, 32, 34, 36–37, 43
magma chambers, 5
magnesium, 17, 20, 42
mantle, 17, 28, 30, 33, 38, 43
metamorphic rock, 5, 14, 37
mica, 11, 24
Mid-Atlantic Ridge, 28
minerals, 11–12, 13–14, 16–17, 18, 20, 22, 25, 42

obsidian, 26, 43–44

olivine, 17, 20, 22
oxygen, 15

pahoehoe lava flows, 8, 25
"parent rock," 13
pegmatite, 23–24, 43
peridotite, 44
petrologists, 13
phaneritic rock. *See* coarse-grained rock.
pillow lava flows, 8
plagioclase, 7, 11–13
plate boundaries, 28
plates. *See* tectonic plates.
plutonic rock, 6, 18, 21, 24
pumice, 19, 26, 32, 41
pyroclastic flow, 7, 8, 9, 32, 37
pyroxene, 17, 20, 22

quarries, 39
quartz, 12, 15, 21, 24

remnant ocean basins, 30
rhyolite, 19, 21, 25, 39, 40
Ring of Fire, 31, 32
rock cycle, 36–37

scoria, 19, 26
sedimentary rock, 5, 14, 36–37
silicates, 15, 20, 25, 41
Soufriere Hills volcano, 7
subduction, 28, 30
supervolcanoes, 32–33

tectonic plates, 28–31, 32, 36
tourmaline, 42, 43
transform boundaries, 31

ultramafic magma, 18, 21–22, 33
uses, 39–41, 43–44

volcanic rock, 5, 18, 20–21, 25
volcanoes, 4–5, 8, 18, 30–31, 32, 34, 35,